THE HOLLYWOOD MUSICAL
A PICTURE QUIZ BOOK

THE HOLLYWOOD MUSICAL
A PICTURE QUIZ BOOK

WITH 215 STILLS FROM CULVER PICTURES, INC.

BY

STANLEY APPELBAUM

Dover Publications, Inc.
New York

Preface & Acknowledgments

Film musicals of many types from 1927 to 1960 are included in this quiz book, in which all the questions are keyed to stills. The stills and questions are arranged in sections according to performers, composers and other categories.

In the selection of the stills, more space has been allotted to musicals specially written or largely readapted for the screen than to straight film versions of Broadway successes. Wherever possible, an attempt has been made to show musical numbers actually being performed, and to reproduce stills that have not been published frequently in the past. Hopefully these illustrations will continue to provide entertainment and information even after the first pleasure of the quiz is past.

All references to the stills are in **boldface** numbers.

To add to the usefulness of the book, the answer section includes the full title of each film, the director, year of release, identification of as many of the performers in the still as possible, and names of the stars even when they do not appear in the still.

Sometimes individual players or movies appear in more than one section of the book, or in a perhaps unexpected section. The Index of Performers and Index of Films will help you trace your favorites.

Wholehearted thanks are due to Culver Pictures, who lent every one of the stills in this book and were unstinting in their encouragement and cooperation. Mr. Roberts Jackson was a cheerful and knowing guide through Culver's incredibly vast picture holdings.

Glossy prints for every illustration included here are available through Culver Pictures, 660 First Avenue, New York, N.Y. 10016.

Reviewers may use up to three illustrations at no charge, but are requested to credit the illustrations to Culver Pictures.

Published in Canada by General Publishing Company, Ltd., 30 Lesmill Road, Don Mills, Toronto, Ontario.
Published in the United Kingdom by Constable and Company, Ltd., 10 Orange Street, London WC 2.

The Hollywood Musical: A Picture Quiz Book is a new work, first published by Dover Publications, Inc., in 1974.

International Standard Book Number: 0-486-23008-2

Manufactured in the United States of America
Dover Publications, Inc.
180 Varick Street
New York, N.Y. 10014

Contents

Al Jolson

1–4
Jolson in four major films
between 1927 and 1935

———

1. Name this 1927 film that was a breakthrough for musicals and for the talkies in general. Who was Jolson's leading lady, shown with him here? What studio produced the film? Who had played the Jolson role on the stage and was originally slated to recreate it in the movie version?

2. What was this 1933 film in which Jolson played the "King of Central Park"? Who is the important comedian seen with him in the still? Who played the mayor of New York? What was the chief song in the Rodgers and Hart score?

3. Here Al owns the night spot that gives the picture its name. What is it? Who played the dancing partners seen taking their bow? Who played the bandleader visible in the background? Who choreographed the big production numbers?

4. Which of these actresses was Jolson's wife in real life? (This was the only film in which they were teamed.) Who is the other actress in the still? What great female vocalist was also in the cast? Which of the following songs did *not* appear in this film? (a) "She's a Latin from Manhattan"; (b) "Why Do I Dream Those Dreams?"; (c) "About a Quarter to Nine."

988-16

Judy Garland

5–11
A spectrum of Judy
from 1937 to 1954

————

5. The "Everybody Sing" number from ——? What wonderful performer is seen here as Judy's mother? Who were the stars of the film? What was Judy's sensational number, which she had originally performed at an actor's birthday party?

6. What was this film in which Judy took a hand in the love life of her glamorous widowed mother? Identify the players in the still. Who was the male lead? In what other film did the same actress play Judy's mother?

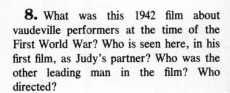

7. What were these little people called? What was the name of this good witch, and who played the role? What was the name of the character portrayed by Judy? Who wrote the songs?

8. What was this 1942 film about vaudeville performers at the time of the First World War? Who is seen here, in his first film, as Judy's partner? Who was the other leading man in the film? Who directed?

9

Judy Garland
continued

9. Identify the players and the film. Who wrote the score, which included "Be a Clown"? Who directed?

10. Who are the performers seen here as Judy's older sister and as "the boy next door" in this 1944 musical? Who played the youngest sister? What song from this film made the biggest hit?

11. Who wrote the new songs for this highly dramatic musical? Who was the leading man, shown in the still? Who directed? Who were the stars of the 1937 nonmusical version of the film?

Fred Astaire

12–17
An assortment of Astaire

___

12. What was this first film of his in which he merely partnered the heroine toward the end of the picture? Identify her. Who was the leading man? What important song was introduced in this movie?

13. Even in this film (what was it?) it was the couple in the center of the still who were the stars (who are they?), but Astaire had a sparkling new partner (who was she, and what major dance-song did they introduce?). Who wrote the score?

14. A Technicolor balletic film that was far ahead of its time. Who is Astaire's partner? Who was the inventive director?

15. Identify this film and the principals, who are gathered together to sing "That's Entertainment." Who wrote the songs, which were mostly from stage musicals of the Thirties?

Fred Astaire

continued

16. What Gershwin song are Astaire and Rogers performing in this roller-skating number, and which of their films is it from? What other Astaire film had a score specially composed by Gershwin, and who was his leading lady in it?

17. This novelty treatment of "Clap Yo' Hands" appeared in a 1957 film named for another Gershwin song of the Twenties. Identify the film and the lady, who is equally renowned as performer, choreographer and author of the "Eloise" books for children.

Gene Kelly

18 & 19
From two of his
most successful films

———

18. What is this film, of which Kelly is here performing the title song? In what film did the song originally appear? With whom did Kelly share direction of the film?

19. Another film with a score made up of Gershwin standards. The climax was this long ballet to a piece of music that gave the picture its name. What song did Kelly perform in the film with a group of children? Who sang "I'll Build a Stairway to Paradise" in the film? Who directed?

Dick Powell & Ruby Keeler

20–23
Four of their films,
as a team and separately

———

20. What was their West Point musical, shown here? Name three of the other six films they did together.

21. Who is Powell's wading partner in this 1937 film directed by Busby Berkeley? Name the movie, which opened with the song "Hooray for Hollywood."

22. Lee Dixon is Ruby's type-dancing partner here. What is the film, what song is being performed, and who wrote the song?

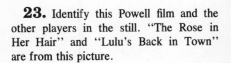

23. Identify this Powell film and the other players in the still. "The Rose in Her Hair" and "Lulu's Back in Town" are from this picture.

Frank Sinatra

24–27
Four moments in his
musical film career

---

24. Can you locate Sinatra here? (He is obviously not one of the stars, but still only a vocalist with the bandleader shown in the center.) Identify the five principals in the center. Name the film.

25. His first major film role. Who is at the piano, and to whom is he singing "I Couldn't Sleep a Wink Last Night"? Who was the male lead, and what was the picture?

26. "I Fall in Love Too Easily" came from this 1945 movie. Name the film and the other two principals shown in the still.

27. Sinatra as Nathan Detroit in the musical based on Damon Runyon characters. What is the film? Who played the role in the original stage production? Who is seen here in her original role of Adelaide? Who composed the score?

Shirley Temple

28 & 29
Two of her classics from 1934,
the year of her great success

_____

28. The "Baby, Take a Bow" number that catapulted her to fame. What was this film about a government bureau of entertainment? Who is seen here as "Daddy"?

29. Who is the "older woman" in this clash of personalities? Which Shirley Temple film is this? What was her big song in it?

KF. 113

Busby Berkeley

30–38
Berkeley as choreographer
and director

──────

30. In which film did this human harp number appear? Who were the (non-musical) stars?

Busby Berkeley
continued

31. What song is being performed in this number? What is the film? What song was used for the finale?

32. Name the film. Who sang the song around which this number was built? Who were the stars of the film?

33. This number appeared in a film that Berkeley directed. Who were the stars? Who were the soloists in the final number?

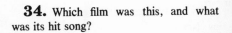

34. Which film was this, and what was its hit song?

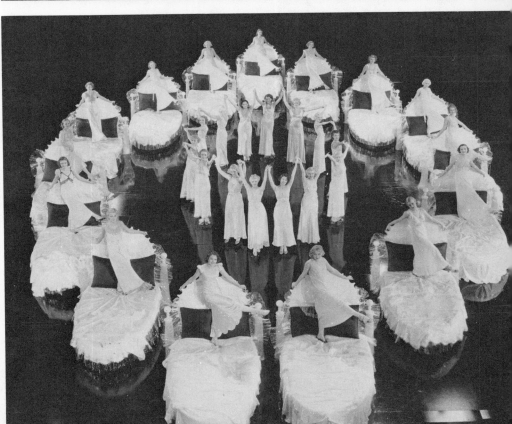

Busby Berkeley

continued

35. In this epoch-making 1933 back-stage musical, who is seen (at the right) as the director of the show and (next to him) as the leading lady of the show? What is her big number in the film? When this leading lady bows out, who gets her part?

36. A 1943 musical directed by Berkeley. Name the film, the soloist shown, and the song she is performing. What female vocalist had the leading role?

37. Comedy in classic Berkeleys. From the same film as **31**. Who were these purveyors of laughs?

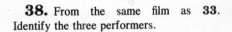

38. From the same film as **33**. Identify the three performers.

Bing Crosby

39–42
Four films,
1933 through 1944

———

39. Who is seen here as Bing's leading lady in this 1933 film, which contained his great song hit "Temptation"? Who played the role of Bing's brunette temptress?

40. Name the film and identify the other performers shown.

935-11

41. This was the first of a series of musical romps with the same starring trio —Bing and who else? Which one of the series is this?

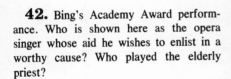

42. Bing's Academy Award performance. Who is shown here as the opera singer whose aid he wishes to enlist in a worthy cause? Who played the elderly priest?

43

44

Jeanette MacDonald & Nelson Eddy

43–46
Four of their films,
as a team and separately

———

43. Name this 1936 film set in Canada. What is the famous duet they sing in it? Who created the two leading roles on the stage? Who played Jeanette's brother, who runs afoul of the Mounties?

44. Who is the gentleman masquerading as a hairdresser in order to be near Jeanette? Name this 1930 film directed by Ernst Lubitsch. What great song does Jeanette sing on a train after she has left her bridegroom waiting at the church?

45. Who is Eddy's leading lady in this film with a Russian setting? What was the name of the inn that gave the film its title?

46. What was this film in which Jeanette was a dancer and a spy? Who was her leading man? Who wrote the score? What song was not in the original 1912 stage production, but became the hit of the film?

Maurice Chevalier

47–50
Stills from some
of his greatest
triumphs

————

47. The finale of one of the great film revues. Name the movie. Name the song being performed. What was Chevalier's other big song in this all-star opus?

48. Who is Chevalier's vis-à-vis in this sketch on the origin of the apache dance? In what film did it appear?

49. Who directed this 1934 version of Lehár's most famous operetta? Who is seen here in the title role? What great director had done a silent version of the story in 1925?

50. Though a mere tailor in this film, Maurice is here impersonating an apache at a fancy dress ball. Who was his leading lady in this 1932 musical with a Rodgers and Hart score? In which films did Chevalier introduce the following? (a) "Louise"; (b) "Mimi"; (c) "My Ideal."

Bandleaders

51–60
Identify the major bandleader
in each still, then try your hand
at the additional questions

---

51. Name this film with a military
academy setting, and identify the singing
and dancing comedienne seen beside the
bandleader.

52. Jack Benny and Ida Lupino
starred in this 1937 musical, which featured several noted cartoonists and illus-
trators. Can you name the film? Who is
the lady on the keg?

53. The bandleader in this still from *Hollywood Hotel* is the clarinetist, but the drummer was to have a band of his own. Who is he? (In this film the bandleader in **51** was still a trumpeter with the clarinetist's aggregation.)

54. The film is *Stormy Weather*, a 1943 showcase of black talent. In what 1932 film did this bandleader perform "Kicking the Gong Around"?

55. Can you name the baby-voiced soprano chucking the bandleader under the chins? The title of this 1930 film revue was the same as the "royal" title given to this great baton-wielder. What was it? What major baritone made his feature debut in this movie as one of the Rhythm Boys who sang with the band?

56. Name the comedian at the right and the entertainer in the center, best known as a newspaper columnist. What was this 1937 musical, in which Alice Faye was the female lead?

57. The bandleader is the one holding the clarinet in his left hand. Identify his two famous vocalists (the blond and the man with the soda bottle) and the singing star of the film (the brunette). This is the "I Remember You" number—from what film? Who sang "Arthur Murray Taught Me Dancing in a Hurry" in this picture (her film debut)?

58. The bandleader is at the far left. Identify all the other performers seated at the table, and name the film.

59. Name the dancer. What was this 1943 film, the source of the song "Happiness Is Just a Thing Called Joe"?

60. Name the singers. The band and the vocalists appeared in several films; this one is *You Were Never Lovelier*. Who were the stars and who wrote the main score?

Female Vocalists

61–94
A generous selection of
the great ladies of song
in filmland

———

61 & 62. Name the blond singer
and these two early films of hers. Identify
the other performers. Which one of the
people in **62** introduced "I'm in the Mood
for Love" in that film?

63 & 64. A top star recreating two of her greatest stage roles. Name her and the films, and identify as many of the other players as you can. Who wrote the score of **64**? Who wrote the stage score of **63**, only part of which was used in the film? Who had created the role of the gangster masquerading as a clergyman? Who was the male lead in **63**?

65 & 66. Who is this great singer, seen here in films dating from 1929 and 1943? (**66** is from the same film as **59**.) What film is shown in **65** (the source of "Am I Blue?")?

Female Vocalists
continued

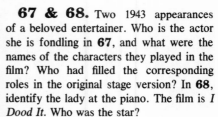

67 & 68. Two 1943 appearances of a beloved entertainer. Who is the actor she is fondling in **67**, and what were the names of the characters they played in the film? Who had filled the corresponding roles in the original stage version? In **68**, identify the lady at the piano. The film is *I Dood It.* Who was the star?

69 & 70. A bright light of vaudeville and revue in two of her infrequent screen appearances. In **69** she sang "Cooking Breakfast for the One I Love" (the breakfast scene is shown in the still). In **70** she appeared as herself in a tribute to a great showman. Who is she? What are the two films?

"God! That you should die for me!" 1225--

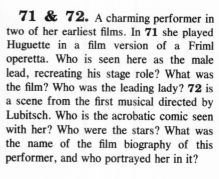

71 & 72. A charming performer in two of her earliest films. In **71** she played Huguette in a film version of a Friml operetta. Who is seen here as the male lead, recreating his stage role? What was the film? Who was the leading lady? **72** is a scene from the first musical directed by Lubitsch. Who is the acrobatic comic seen with her? Who were the stars? What was the name of the film biography of this performer, and who portrayed her in it?

73 & 74. The advent of the talkies revealed that this silent film star had a very pleasant soprano. **73** shows the title-song scene from a 1929 success based on a stage musical. Who is the leading man? **74** is from an original screen operetta of 1930. The leading man, shown in the still, was a Metropolitan Opera baritone from 1927 to 1931. Who is he? What was the film?

Female Vocalists

continued

75 & 76. A supreme pin-up girl as she appeared in 1936 and in 1947. How many of the six front-line singers can you identify in still **75**, from *Pigskin Parade*? What great musical star made her feature debut in that picture? Who is the male performer in **76**, and what is the film?

77 & 78. An outstanding star of stage operetta and musical comedy (best remembered for *Pal Joey*) in two 1930 films, *Viennese Nights* (**77**) and *Golden Dawn* (**78**). Who wrote the score for **77**? (The score of **78** was by Emmerich Kálmán.) Who are the male performers? (The one in **77** sang in several musicals, but is best known as a non musical romantic leading man.)

Female Vocalists
continued

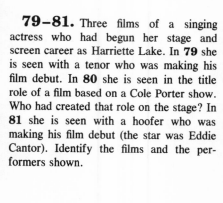

79–81. Three films of a singing actress who had begun her stage and screen career as Harriette Lake. In **79** she is seen with a tenor who was making his film debut. In **80** she is seen in the title role of a film based on a Cole Porter show. Who had created that role on the stage? In **81** she is seen with a hoofer who was making his film debut (the star was Eddie Cantor). Identify the films and the performers shown.

81

82

82. One of the greatest popular singers (she was portrayed by Doris Day in her screen biography) is seen here in a multi-star 1934 film, *The Gift of Gab*, together with the Texan tenor who popularized such songs as "My Blue Heaven" and "Ain't She Sweet." Identify.

Female Vocalists
continued

83. Who is the raucous and rowdy vocalist, who are the comics, and what is this zany 1941 film in which their talents were pooled?

84. Another peppy and zippy singer in a film version of a stage musical. Who is she? Name two out of the three men. What was the film? Who had the leading role on Broadway? Who was the composer? What two historical characters were portrayed by two of the people in the still?

85. The film is *Heads Up*, based on a Rodgers and Hart show. Who is the baby-talk female vocalist? What cartoon character was based on her personality? Who is the male comic?

86. Who is the popular soprano seen here in a Fannie Hurst story about a radio star who defends farmers against unscrupulous villains?

87. Name this British singer, a great success in German film musicals, seen here in an American film in which puppets played a great part. What was the film, and who was the leading man?

88. This operatic soprano is linked in memory with this film, a biography of Johann Strauss, Jr. Name her, name the film, name the French actor at the left who portrayed Strauss, and name the two players in the right foreground.

89. Identify these talented singers and dancers. What was this film, which included the songs "On the Boardwalk at Atlantic City" and "You Make Me Feel So Young"?

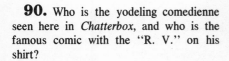

90. Who is the yodeling comedienne seen here in *Chatterbox*, and who is the famous comic with the "R. V." on his shirt?

Female Vocalists
continued

91. An East European accent was a feature of this comedienne's style. The radio comic at the right was famous for his line "Wanna buy a duck?" Who are they? This is the varsity football musical that included "Stay As Sweet As You Are." What was it? Who was the male singing star?

92. Name this vivacious singer who introduced "The Lullaby of Broadway" and "The Lady in Red" in Busby Berkeley films. Who is the tenor seen with her here in *Melody for Two*?

93. Who is this female vocalist, and what was this film in which she made her screen debut?

94. This was the film debut of the soprano at the left. Can you name this 1944 movie and the actress at the right?

Male Vocalists

95–114
Outstanding tenors and baritones
(and one soprano)

---

95 & 96. Still **95** is from the singing bandleader's first starring film, named after one of his biggest song hits. His leading lady was Loretta Young's sister. Who are they? What was the film? Name the other performers shown in **96**, from his film *Sweet Music*.

97 & 98. Name this talented singer and dancer, shown here as he appeared in early and advanced adolescence. Who are the other performers in **97**, and what was the movie (his first feature film)? Who is the female live wire seen with him in **98**? They were teamed in several pictures in the Forties; this scene is from *Chip Off the Old Block.*

Male Vocalists
continued

99 & 100. "Ukulele Ike" was the nickname of the singer seen at the right in **99** and at the left in **100**. After long stage experience, including the Ziegfeld Follies, he was in the movies for years, and lent his voice to the cartoon character Jiminy Cricket in Disney's *Pinocchio*. What is his name? Identify as many others in these two stills as you can —especially the singer at the left in **99** (the man who first sang "Over There" in public in 1917) and the man sitting on the card table in **100** (that actor's first film).

101 & 102. From which two films starring this versatile performer are these stills? Who are his dancing partners? Hint: **102** was choreographed by Roland Petit of Paris, and the ballerina was the star of his company. Who wrote the score of **102**?

Male Vocalists

continued

103 & 104. A great singing comic in two of his earliest sound films. **103** was a movie version of a great stage success of his, and is famous as the only movie that Ziegfeld ever took a personal part in producing—and the first movie with Busby Berkeley choreography. Name it. Identify the comedienne wearing the kimono in **104**.

105. Rouben Mamoulian directed this musical satire with the well-known tenor at the right. Who is he, who is seen here as his leading lady, and what was the film?

106. The popular baritone at the right was killed in a freak accident in the same year that this film was released. Who was he? What was the film? Can you identify the leading lady, an important singer on stage and screen?

107. This baritone first became popular as the partner of a goofy comedian, but has done much work on his own. Here he appears in the film version of a Jule Styne show. The actress was recreating her Broadway role. Who are they? What is the film?

108. Identify the tenor and the other performers. Can you tell which of his films this is from?

109. A film version of a Broadway musical that was in turn based on an opera. Who is seen here as a deserter from the army, and who is the siren that made him turn bad?

110. Who is the baritone seen here in *Music in My Heart*? Who is the well-known orchestra leader?

Male Vocalists
continued

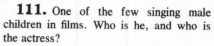

111. One of the few singing male children in films. Who is he, and who is the actress?

112. An Irish tenor and a universal mother figure. The film is *Mother's Boy*. Who are they?

113

113. One of the phenomena of the Fifties and Sixties, in his second film, *Loving You.* Who is he? What was his first film?

114

114. The "Song of the Dawn" number from *King of Jazz.* Who is the singing star, and what was the other very famous song he introduced in this film?

Dancers

115–120
Tap, ballroom, ballet

115 & 116. A spirited dancer in two roles. In **115** she appears in a dance interlude from a 1948 film that starred Frank Sinatra and Kathryn Grayson. What is the film? Who are the performers? What is the big song from this movie? **116** shows the "Prehistoric Man" number in the American Museum of Natural History in New York. What was this film about three sailors on shore leave? Who composed the Broadway show on which it was based? Who played the other two sailors in the film?

117. The *prima donna assoluta* of British film musicals, as she appeared in *Head Over Heels*. What was her best-remembered film, in which she performed "Dancing on the Ceiling"?

118. Identify this gentleman, possibly the most prestigious tap dancer of all time, seen here in *Hooray for Love*. What famous black pianist-composer also appeared in the film?

Dancers

continued

119. An outstanding dancer as he appeared in *Harold Teen.* Identify him and the actress.

120. One of the big dance numbers from a 1954 musical that immediately became a classic of the genre. Who were the two singing stars? For dance fans: can you identify the three leaping men?

George Gershwin Scores

121–126

121 & 122. Gershwin died before completing the score of this film, which contains two of his most popular songs. What are they? Who is the ballerina in **121** (her choreography was by Balanchine), and who are the performers on either side of her? Who is the tenor in **122**, and who is the Metropolitan Opera soprano, making her film debut in this picture?

George Gershwin Scores
continued

123. Who are the stars of this 1943 version of a Gershwin show (there had been a 1932 film version)? What is the film?

124. The first and most striking example of a posthumous film score—new songs adapted from Gershwin manuscripts, including "For You, For Me, For Evermore." What was this film? Identify the players. What was the leading lady's profession in the picture (it was one of the newest at the time of the story)?

125. Name this film that used a score of Gershwin standards, and the actress who appears in it as a fashion-model-in-spite-of-herself.

126. This was the film biography of Gershwin. What was it called? Who is the actor (in the center) who played the composer? Who else is seen in the still?

Jerome Kern Scores

127–134

127. The perils of a garret-to-garret visit over the rooftops. Who are these singers in this movie version of a major Kern show? Which of the following songs is *not* included in this film? (a) "The Night Was Made for Love"; (b) "She Didn't Say Yes"; (c) "I Watch the Love Parade"; (d) "I've Told Ev'ry Little Star."

128. Another Kern stage show transferred to the screen. Identify the two stars (the dark-haired woman and the man in the light suit). Name the film.

129. This was the first film of this celebrated French coloratura soprano, in which she sang "The Jockey on the Carrousel." Who played her husband, an American composer (at the right)? Who played their downstairs neighbor (at the left), a vaudevillian with a trained seal act? What was the title song?

130. What was this musical based on a Kern show set in the 1890s (the source of "Why Was I Born?")? Irene Dunne starred in the film; who had the main role on the stage? Identify the performers at the table in the foreground.

Jerome Kern Scores
continued

131 & 132. Two scenes from the "definitive" 1936 film version (the others date from 1929 and 1951) of Kern's most prestigious show. Name the performers in the stills. Who repeated his Broadway role of Cap'n Andy in this 1936 movie?

HAWKS' COTTON PALACE REFINED REPERTORY STARRING GAYLORD RAVENAL (OF TENNESSEE)

HAWKS' COTTON PALACE REFINED REPERTORY STARRING MAGNOLIA HAWKS

133. A 1944 musical named for one of the songs in the Kern score. Who is the soprano? In what film made in the same year did she introduce "Spring Will Be a Little Late This Year"? Identify the two actors in the foreground.

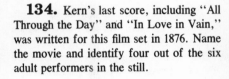

134. Kern's last score, including "All Through the Day" and "In Love in Vain," was written for this film set in 1876. Name the movie and identify four out of the six adult performers in the still.

Richard Rodgers Scores

135–139

135. Rodgers and Hart were already writing complete film scores in 1931. This original screenplay involved a very rich young lady and a team of riveters. Can you name the film? How many of the principals in the still can you identify?

136. The film version of a highly successful Rodgers and Hart show, which includes "Falling in Love with Love" and "This Can't Be Love." Name it and identify at least three of the performers.

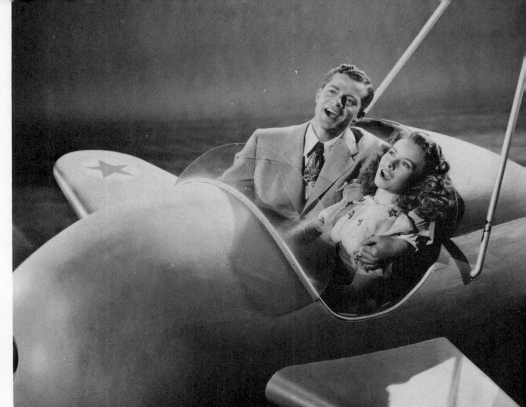

137. What Rodgers and Hammerstein song are these performers singing? Who are they? What is the film? Which song from this film won an Academy Award? Who starred in the 1933 nonmusical film with this title and story? Who starred in the 1962 musical remake?

138. In what country does this Rodgers and Hammerstein musical take place? Identify the performers. Who played their roles on Broadway?

Richard Rodgers Scores
continued

139. In what state does this Rodgers and Hammerstein musical take place? Again, identify the performers and tell who played their roles on Broadway.

Irving Berlin Scores

140-142

140. Many of the musical selections in this 1929 King Vidor classic were traditional, but Irving Berlin contributed a couple of fine songs. What is the film? Who played the hero, seen here?

141. The song being performed in this still was first sung by this very man in a soldiers' show in 1918. He sang it again in a 1942 show, and then in this film version of that show. Name the film, the song, the performer and the 1918 show.

142. Berlin contributed three new songs to this 1930 showcase for this male vocalist. The title song, being performed here, has never lost its appeal. What is the film? Who is the singer?

Cole Porter Scores

143–148

143 & 144. The three superb performers in these two stills appeared in the film with the best original Porter score, including "Easy to Love" and "I've Got You Under My Skin." Name the film and identify the performers. Who sang "I've Got You . . ." in the film?

145. Which film with a Porter score had this setting for its grand finale? Who is the soloist? Who was her leading man in the film?

1011-97

Cole Porter Scores

continued

146 & 147. Both these Eleanor
Powell dance numbers were in one Porter-
score film, set partially in West Point and
partially in a Ruritanian kingdom. What
was the film, who was the leading man,
and what were the two most important
songs?

148. Porter, too, had to endure his screen biography. What was it called? Name the performers in the still. The lady with the music played herself, auditioning for a Porter show. What was this show, in which she became famous?

DeSylva, Brown & Henderson Scores

149–153
A selection of films featuring
music by Bud DeSylva, Lew Brown
and Ray Henderson

---

149. From the first (1930) film version of their most successful Broadway show. The man in the striped sweater was in the original cast (and in the original cast of *The New Moon*, as well). The actress had appeared in silent films and was one of the most important people in early musicals. The angry-looking man became a major director of westerns, with such credits as *Broken Arrow* and *3:10 to Yuma*. Who are they? What is the film? Who starred in the 1947 remake?

150 & 151. These two stills are from a clever 1930 musical taking place in New York City in 1980 (**151** shows the chief model set). Maureen O'Sullivan and El Brendel had major roles. What is the film? Who are the singers in **150** performing ''Never Swat a Fly''?

**DeSylva, Brown
& Henderson Scores**

continued

152 & 153. Two numbers from the trio's finest original film score. In **152** the heroine is performing the title song. Who is she? Who was her leading man? In what film were they first teamed? Can you name the song being performed in **153**?

Comedy in Musicals

154–163
Some of the great
figures of fun—when musicals
were musical *comedies*

154 & 155. Who is this Italian comedian? In what picture did he introduce "Inka Dinka Doo"? What great man of the American theater is seen with him in **154**? What was this film in which they appeared together? Who was the leading lady? Try to identify the other unhappy fathers in **155**, from *George White's Scandals* (1934). What major female vocalist made her film debut in that picture?

Comedy in Musicals
continued

156. Name the comedian at the left, seen with George Ovey and Polly Walker in the 1930 film version of a Vincent Youmans show. What is the film?

157. A scene from the 1929 Warner Bros. all-star revue, *Show of Shows.* How many of these comics can you name? (The lady with the pearl necklace is a must for identification.)

158. Who are these funny people, seen here in *Flying High* (1931)?

159. The disheveled pair in the center were teamed in *Rio Rita* (stage and 1929 film version) and then again and again in the Thirties. Who are they? Can you name this specific musical? Can you identify the actress with the fan and the actress who is pointing?

Comedy in Musicals
continued

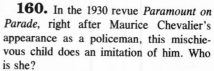

160. In the 1930 revue *Paramount on Parade*, right after Maurice Chevalier's appearance as a policeman, this mischievous child does an imitation of him. Who is she?

161–163. *The* movie lunatics, the Marx Brothers, and some of the singers associated with their films. Which picture is **161** from? Who is the lady attempting to rise from the chair? The couple in **162**, then famous on the stage, appeared in the Marx Brothers' first film in 1929. What was the film, who are they, and what Irving Berlin song did they render? What Marx Brothers film is shown in **163**? Name the singers.

Brothers & Sisters

164–167
Family teams in musicals

—————

164. Name the brothers. Name the film. What band was providing the music for this dance? Who was the solo vocalist?

165. "Coffee in the Morning and Kisses at Night." Who are the vocal sisters? What is the film?

166. Don't forget to name the couple in the background when you identify the singing foursome. The picture is *Strictly Dynamite*.

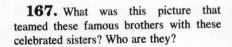

167. What was this picture that teamed these famous brothers with these celebrated sisters? Who are they?

Biographies

168–171
Some Hollywood versions
of great lives
in music

___

168. Who was portrayed by this actress, and what was the film called? What great male dancer is also in the still? Who wrote the song that gave the film its title, and in what show did the subject of the biography perform it? Did the subject of the biography ever make films herself?

169. What stars of vaudeville and revue were the subjects of *Shine On Harvest Moon*? Which two performers shown here portrayed them? Who are the other players in the still?

170. What was the name of this biography of the songwriters Bert Kalmar and Harry Ruby? In what film did the title song originally appear? Identify the players in the foreground.

171. She isn't used to horseradish. Whose life story was this? Who played the main role? Identify the heroine.

Opera Stars in Musicals

172–175
Glories of
the Metropolitan Opera
in musical films

—————

172. Who is the outstanding Irish tenor? Who is the Irish girl who first appeared in this 1930 film? Name the movie.

173. This reconstruction of early recording techniques occurs in a film that starred Kathryn Grayson and June Allyson. Name the movie and identify the *heldentenor* in the still.

174. Though there were songs in his pictures with Dietrich, this was Josef von Sternberg's only film operetta, based on the romance of Franz Josef and Elisabeth of Austria. Who is the soprano? Who is seen here as the young Franz Josef? What was the film? Who wrote the score? What was the most popular song (a revision of a song from a 1919 stage operetta by the same composer)?

175. The same soprano as in **174**, teamed with an operatic baritone. Who is he? What was this 1930 film that they made together, using the score of a stage operetta with a different plot? What two singers starred in the 1940 film version, which reverted to the original plot? Who was the composer?

Specialties & Offbeat Films

176–182
A few unusual
or striking aspects of
musical film history

176. This was the first musical to win an Academy Award as best picture of the year. What was it? In what year was it released? Name the three principals shown. Which of the following songs did *not* appear in this film? (a) "You Were Meant for Me"; (b) "Happy Days Are Here Again"; (c) "The Wedding of the Painted Doll."

177. Costumes and sets were by Erté in this elaborate publicity shot for a 1929 all-star MGM revue. Can you identify the pearl girl inside the shell? Can you name the film?

178 & 179. Some of the best musical scores in the Thirties and Forties were to be found in Disney cartoons. In fact, the song from **178** became an international best seller. What was the song? What was the cartoon? What actor lent his voice to Timothy Mouse in **179**? Name the film.

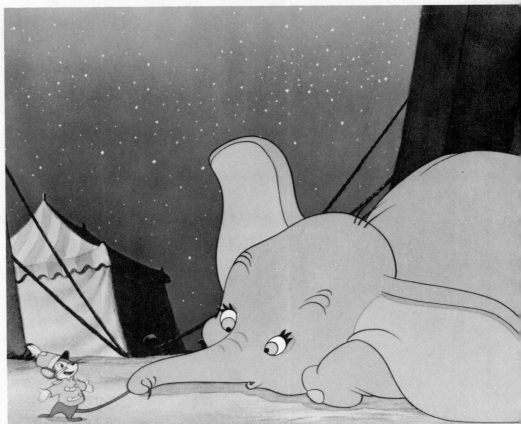

469.

Specialties & Offbeat Films

continued

180. A musical directed by Cecil B. DeMille! This is a scene from the masquerade party held on a moored dirigible. What was the film? Name at least two of the three principals in the still.

181. A musical with Portuguese dialogue, and without stars, that won the

hearts of the world. What was it? In what city was it filmed?

182. An actress not generally remembered as a musical performer, as she appeared in the 1929 film version of *The Desert Song*. Who is she? Who played "The Red Shadow" in the three film versions of this operetta (1929, 1943 and 1953)?

Production Numbers

183–189
Spectacular settings for
large performing forces

---

183. Busby Berkeley strikes again. This is the intimate group in the "Mu-chacha" number in the same picture that includes "The Lady in Red." What is the picture? (The star appears at the lower left.)

184. This is the "A Pretty Girl Is Like a Melody" number in a biographical film that won an Oscar as best picture of 1936. What is the movie?

Production Numbers

continued

185 & 186. Two production numbers from Eleanor Powell films. Name the pictures. Who was her leading man in each of the films?

185

186

Production Numbers

continued

187. This film is the source of "The Boulevard of Broken Dreams." Can you identify the star, who is not well known as a musical performer?

188. Another biographical film. What was it? Who was the subject? What song is being performed? Identify at least three of the players in the foreground.

748-319

189

Production Numbers

continued

189. This 1929 film, the source of "True Blue Lou," was based on the successful play *Burlesque*. The stars were Nancy Carroll and the man made up as a clown. Who is he? What was the film?

Broadway Stars in Early Musicals

190–195
Exciting entertainers who did not enjoy flourishing Hollywood careers

190. Who are these two stage luminaries, seen here in a 1930 film version of a 1928 Cole Porter show (with the Porter songs replaced by others!)? What was the film?

191. Identify this blond, pride and joy of Florenz Ziegfeld in his Follies and several book shows. Who is the comedian with her, and what is this 1931 film in which they appeared together?

Broadway Stars in Early Musicals
continued

192. Who is this great British songstress, seen here in *The Battle of Paris*? Identify the two comedians.

193. This lady created the role of Rio Rita on the stage. Who is she? This film is the source of "Should I (Reveal)" and "A Bundle of Old Love Letters." What is it?

194. The lady was the original Magnolia Hawks in *Show Boat* on Broadway. The gentleman was the original leading man in *Rio Rita*. They are seen together here in *Married in Hollywood*. Who are they?

195. A formidable array of stage talent was assembled for this 1929 film, which gave its name to a sporadic series of musicals. The gentleman with the guitar sang "Tip Toe Through the Tulips with Me" in the film. The blond was a noted siren and clotheshorse. The famous dancer on the stool had introduced the Black Bottom. The singing comedienne in the black dress had introduced major Gershwin songs in editions of *George White's Scandals*. Identify as many of these people as you can, and name the film, which was also the source of "Painting the Clouds with Sunshine."

Various Personalities

196–209
Some of the
performers who lent their
talents to film musicals

—————

196. Who is this sex goddess? What is the title song?

197. Exceptional neither as singers nor as dancers, still these performers had a *je ne sais quoi* that made their presence in musicals welcome. Who are they? What was this film in which they appeared together? Who had played the leading role on the stage?

198. This historical fantasy had a score by Kurt Weill. What was it called? Who are the performers seen in this very early view of Manhattan?

199. Who was this swimmer around whom many an MGM musical was framed in the Forties? Identify her leading man, who alternated musical appearances with work in straight films.

Various Personalities

continued

200–202. A highly personable actress in three of her early musicals. Name her and try to identify the other players. **200** is from the film version of a DeSylva, Brown and Henderson show about golfing, the source of "Button Up Your Overcoat." **202** is the source of "Sing, You Sinners." What are these films?

203. The actress at the right was one of the big names in silent pictures, starring in such films as *Ella Cinders* and *Lilac Time.* Here she is seen in the 1929 film *Footlights and Fools.* Who is she? Who is the leading man, shown in the still?

Various Personalities
continued

204 & 205. This actress, also a silent star, made some engaging musicals. Can you identify her?

206. The film is *Dancing Sweeties.* How many of the performers can you identify?

207. Who is the important orchestral conductor seen here? In what picture did he share the screen with Mickey Mouse? Who was the young soprano starred in *100 Men and a Girl,* from which this still is taken? Who is the actor at the right?

Various Personalities
continued

208. Who plays the glamorous star visiting a military academy for publicity? What is the film? What is the school song performed in the film by the young man at the right? Identify the actor in the dark suit, who created the role of Wintergreen in *Of Thee I Sing*.

209. A joyous finish to the book. An Academy Award winner for best picture, direction, art direction, color, costumes, editing, scoring, best song, and writing (screenplay based on material from another medium). Identify the players in the still. What grand old man of musicals also appeared in it? Who wrote the songs? Who wrote the story on which it was based? Who directed? What was the Academy Award winning song? What was the title of the film?

Answers

*Stills **A** through **F** appear on the covers.*

A. *Gold Diggers of 1937* (1936; directed by Lloyd Bacon). Joan Blondell is leading the girls. The male lead was Dick Powell.

B. Jeanette MacDonald and Maurice Chevalier in *The Love Parade*, directed by Ernst Lubitsch.

C. Eddie Cantor, Joan Davis, Constance Moore and George Murphy in *Show Business* (1944; directed by Edwin L. Marin).

D. Gwen Verdon with Tab Hunter in *Damn Yankees* (1958; directed by George Abbott and Stanley Donen).

E. Jimmy Durante, Frank Sinatra, Peter Lawford and Kathryn Grayson in *It Happened in Brooklyn* (directed by Richard Whorf).

F. Jack Haley, Shirley Temple and Alice Faye in *Poor Little Rich Girl* (1936; directed by Irving Cummings).

1. *The Jazz Singer* (directed by Alan Crosland). The actress is May McAvoy. The studio was Warner Bros. The stage star was George Jessel.

2. *Hallelujah, I'm a Bum* (directed by Mervyn LeRoy). The comedian is Harry Langdon. The mayor was played by Frank Morgan. The chief song was "You Are Too Beautiful." The female lead was Madge Evans.

3. *Wonder Bar* (1934; directed by Lloyd Bacon). The performers in the foreground are Ricardo Cortez and Dolores Del Rio; in the background, Dick Powell. The choreographer was Busby Berkeley. Kay Francis was also starred.

4. *Go Into Your Dance* (1935; directed by Archie Mayo). Jolson's wife was Ruby Keeler, at the right in the still. The other actress is Glenda Farrell. The vocalist was Helen Morgan. "Why Do I Dream Those Dreams?" was in *Wonder Bar*.

5. *Broadway Melody of 1938* (1937; directed by Roy Del Ruth). Sophie Tucker played the mother. The stars were Eleanor Powell, Robert Taylor and George Murphy. Judy's big number, originally performed at Clark Gable's birthday party in 1936, was a special arrangement of "You Made Me Love You." The actor at the right in the still is Barnett Parker.

6. *Listen Darling* (1938; directed by Edwin L. Marin). In the still with Judy are Scotty Beckett, Mary Astor and Freddie Bartholomew. The male lead was Walter Pidgeon. Mary Astor also played Judy's mother in *Meet Me in St. Louis*.

7. *The Wizard of Oz* (1939; directed by Victor Fleming). The little people are Munchkins (played by the Singer Midgets). The witch,

played by Billie Burke, was named Glinda. The character portrayed by Judy was called Dorothy. The songs were by Harold Arlen (lyrics by E. Y. Harburg). Other chief performers: Ray Bolger, Jack Haley, Bert Lahr.

8. *For Me and My Gal* (directed by Busby Berkeley). Gene Kelly is in the still. George Murphy was the other leading man.

9. *The Pirate* (1948; directed by Vincente Minnelli). In the still with Judy are Walter Slezak, Gene Kelly, Gladys Cooper. The score was by Cole Porter.

10. *Meet Me in St. Louis* (1944; directed by Vincente Minnelli). Lucille Bremer was the older sister; Tom Drake, the boy next door; Margaret O'Brien, the youngest sister. The "Trolley Song" was the biggest hit.

11. *A Star Is Born* (1954; directed by George Cukor). James Mason was the leading man. The new songs were by Harold Arlen (lyrics by Ira Gershwin). ("Born in a Trunk" was by Leonard Gershe.) The 1937 film starred Janet Gaynor and Fredric March.

12. *Dancing Lady* (1933; directed by Robert Z. Leonard). The heroine is Joan Crawford. The male lead was Clark Gable. The best-remembered song is "Everything I Have Is Yours."

13. *Flying Down to Rio* (1933; directed by Thornton Freeland). The stars were Dolores Del Rio and Gene Raymond. Astaire's new partner was Ginger Rogers, and they introduced "The Carioca." The score was by Vincent Youmans (with Edward Eliscu and Gus Kahn).

14. *Yolanda and the Thief* (1945; directed by Vincente Minnelli). Astaire's partner is Lucille Bremer.

15. *The Band Wagon* (1953; directed by Vincente Minnelli). In the still with Astaire, from left to right, are Oscar Levant, Cyd Charisse, Jack Buchanan and Nanette Fabray. The songs were by Arthur Schwartz (lyrics by Howard Dietz).

16. *Shall We Dance* (1937; directed by Mark Sandrich). The song is "Let's Call the Whole Thing Off." Astaire's other film with a score commissioned from Gershwin was *Damsel in Distress*, with Joan Fontaine.

17. *Funny Face* (directed by Stanley Donen). Kay Thompson is in the still. Audrey Hepburn was the leading lady.

18. *Singin' in the Rain* (1952; co-directed with Stanley Donen). Debbie Reynolds and Donald O'Connor were also starred. The title song first appeared in *The Hollywood Revue of 1929*.

19. *An American in Paris* (1951; directed by Vincente Minnelli). The song with the children was "I Got Rhythm." "I'll Build . . ." was sung by Georges Guétary. Leslie Caron was also starred.

20. *Flirtation Walk* (1934; directed by Frank Borzage). Their other films together were *42nd Street, Gold Diggers of 1933, Footlight Parade, Dames, Shipmates Forever* and *Colleen.*

21. *Hollywood Hotel.* The leading lady, shown in the still, was Rosemary Lane.

22. *Ready, Willing and Able* (1937; directed by Ray Enright). The song is "Too Marvelous for Words," by Richard Whiting (lyrics by Johnny Mercer).

23. *Broadway Gondolier* (1935; directed by Lloyd Bacon). In the still with Powell are Joan Blondell, Adolphe Menjou and Louise Fazenda.

24. *Ship Ahoy* (1942; directed by Edward Buzzell). Sinatra is at the far left. The principals, in the center, are Red Skelton, Eleanor Powell, Tommy Dorsey, Virginia O'Brien and Bert Lahr.

25. *Higher and Higher* (1943; directed by Tim Whelan). At the piano is Dooley Wilson. The actress is Michèle Morgan. The male lead was Jack Haley.

26. *Anchors Aweigh* (directed by George Sidney). Kathryn Grayson and Gene Kelly are shown.

27. *Guys and Dolls* (1955; directed by Joseph L. Mankiewicz). Sam Levene had the role on the stage. Adelaide was played by Vivian Blaine. Words and music were by Frank Loesser.

28. *Stand Up and Cheer* (directed by Hamilton McFadden). James Dunn is in the still. The star was Warner Baxter.

29. *Bright Eyes* (directed by David Butler). The other girl is Jane Withers. The song is "On the Good Ship Lollipop." James Dunn was the male lead.

30. *Fashions of 1934* (1934; directed by William Dieterle). The stars were Bette Davis and William Powell.

31. *Gold Diggers of 1933* (1933; directed by Mervyn LeRoy). This opening number was "The Gold Diggers' Song (We're in the Money)." The finale was "Remember My Forgotten Man." The stars were Joan Blondell, Warren William, Dick Powell and Ruby Keeler.

32. *Footlight Parade* (1933; directed by Lloyd Bacon). "By a Waterfall" was sung by Dick Powell and Ruby Keeler. The stars were James Cagney and Joan Blondell.

33. *Gold Diggers of 1935* (1935). The stars were Dick Powell and Gloria Stuart. The soloists in the final number, "Lullaby of Broadway," were Wini(fred) Shaw and Dick Powell.

34. *Dames* (1934; directed by Ray Enright). The hit song was "I Only Have Eyes for You." The stars were Joan Blondell, Dick Powell and Ruby Keeler.

35. *42nd Street* (directed by Lloyd Bacon). In the still, left to right beginning with the man in the derby: Allen Jenkins, George E. Stone, Bebe Daniels and Warner Baxter. Bebe Daniels' big song is "You're Getting to Be a Habit with Me." She is replaced in the show by Ruby Keeler. The cast also included George Brent, Dick Powell, Una Merkel and Ginger Rogers.

36. *The Gang's All Here.* Carmen Miranda singing "The Lady in the Tutti-Frutti Hat." Alice Faye starred.

37. Aline MacMahon and Guy Kibbee.

38. Hugh Herbert, Glenda Farrell and Adolphe Menjou.

39. *Going Hollywood* (directed by Raoul Walsh). The leading lady was Marion Davies, the temptress was Fifi D'Orsay.

40. *East Side of Heaven* (1939; directed by David Butler). Shown with Bing are Mischa Auer and Joan Blondell.

41. *Road to Singapore* (1940; directed by Victor Schertzinger). The others in the trio are Bob Hope and Dorothy Lamour.

42. *Going My Way* (1944; directed by Leo McCarey). The opera singer is Risë Stevens. The elderly priest was Barry Fitzgerald.

43. *Rose Marie* (directed by W. S. Van Dyke). The famous duet was "The Indian Love Call." The roles were created by Mary Ellis and Dennis King. The brother was played by James Stewart in the film.

44. *Monte Carlo.* The man is Jack Buchanan. The song on the train is "Beyond the Blue Horizon."

45. *Balalaika* (1939; directed by Reinhold Schünzel). The actress is Ilona Massey.

46. *The Firefly* (1937; directed by Robert Z. Leonard). The leading man was Allan Jones. The score was by Rudolf Friml (lyrics by Otto Harbach). The new song was "Donkey Serenade" (by Friml, with Herbert Stothart, Bob Wright and Chet Forrest).

47. *Paramount on Parade* (1930; by several directors, Chevalier's appearances directed by Ernst Lubitsch). The song shown in the still is "Sweeping the Clouds Away." Chevalier also sang "All I Want Is Just One."

48. This is also from *Paramount on Parade.* The actress is Evelyn Brent.

49. *The Merry Widow* (directed by Ernst Lubitsch). Jeanette MacDonald had the title role. Erich von Stroheim did the 1925 version.

50. *Love Me Tonight* (directed by Rouben Mamoulian). Jeanette MacDonald was the leading lady. "Mimi" appeared in this film, "Louise" in *Innocents of Paris*, "My Ideal" in *Playboy of Paris*.

51. Harry James (seen with Nancy Walker) in *Best Foot Forward* (1943; directed by Edward Buzzell). The stars were Lucille Ball and William Gaxton.

52. Louis Armstrong (seen with Martha Raye) in *Artists and Models* (1937; directed by Raoul Walsh).

53. Benny Goodman (seen with Gene Krupa) in *Hollywood Hotel* (1937; directed by Busby Berkeley). The stars were Dick Powell and Rosemary Lane.

54. Cab Calloway. The director was Andrew Stone. The cast also included Ethel Waters, Lena Horne and Bill Robinson. The 1932 film was *The Big Broadcast*.

55. Paul Whiteman (seen with Jeanie Lang) in *King of Jazz* (1930; directed by John Murray Anderson). The baritone was Bing Crosby.

56. Ben Bernie (seen with Walter Winchell and Jack Haley) in *Wake Up and Live* (directed by Sidney Lanfield).

57. Jimmy Dorsey in *The Fleet's In* (1942; directed by Victor Schertzinger). The band vocalists are Helen O'Connell and Bob Eberly. The star is Dorothy Lamour. Betty Hutton sang "Arthur Murray . . . ." The male lead was William Holden.

58. Glenn Miller (seen with Lynn Bari, John Payne, Sonja Henie and Milton Berle) in *Sun Valley Serenade* (1941; directed by H. Bruce Humberstone).

59. Duke Ellington in *Cabin in the Sky* (1943; directed by Vincente Minnelli). The dancer is "Bubbles" (John W. Sublett).

60. Xavier Cugat (seen with Lina Romay and Miguelito Valdez). The 1942 film was directed by William A. Seiter. The stars were Fred Astaire and Rita Hayworth. The score was by Jerome Kern (lyrics by Johnny Mercer).

61 & 62. Alice Faye. In **61** she is seen with Lew Ayres in *She Learned About Sailors* (1934; directed by George Marshall). In **62** she is seen with George Raft, Frances Langford (who sang "I'm in the Mood for Love") and Patsy Kelly in *Every Night at Eight* (1935; directed by Raoul Walsh).

63 & 64. Ethel Merman. In **63** she is seen with Charles Ruggles and Arthur Treacher in *Anything Goes* (1936; directed by Lewis Milestone); Bing Crosby was the male lead; the stage score was by Cole Porter; the gangster role was played by Victor Moore on the stage. In **64** she is seen with George Sanders (far left), Donald O'Connor and Billy De Wolfe (with white ties) in *Call Me Madam* (1953; directed by Walter Lang); score by Irving Berlin.

65 & 66. Ethel Waters. In **65** she is seen in *On with the Show* (directed by Alan Crosland); the cast also included Betty Compson and Joe E. Brown. In **66** she is seen with "Bubbles" (John W. Sublett).

67 & 68. Lena Horne. In **67**, as "Sweet Georgia Brown," she is fondling Eddie Anderson as "Little Joe" (with Kenneth Spencer and Rex Ingram in the background) in *Cabin in the Sky* (1943; directed by Vincente Minnelli); the Horne and Anderson roles were filled by Katherine Dunham and Dooley Wilson on the stage. In **68** Hazel Scott is at the piano. Red Skelton was the star of this 1943 film, also directed by Minnelli.

69 & 70. Fannie Brice. In **69** she is seen with Robert Armstrong in *Be Yourself* (1930; directed by Thornton Freeland). In **70** she is seen with Esther Muir in *The Great Ziegfeld* (1936; directed by Robert Z. Leonard), which starred William Powell, Luise Rainer and Myrna Loy.

71 & 72. Lillian Roth. In **71** she is seen with Dennis King in *The Vagabond King* (1930; directed by Ludwig Berger), in which Jeanette MacDonald was the leading lady. In **72** she is seen with Lupino Lane in *The Love Parade* (1929), in which Jeanette MacDonald and Maurice Chevalier starred. Susan Hayward portrayed Lillian Roth in *I'll Cry Tomorrow*.

73 & 74. Bebe Daniels. In **73** she is seen with John Boles in *Rio Rita* (directed by Luther Reed). In **74** she is seen with Everett Marshall in *Dixiana* (also directed by Reed).

75 & 76. Betty Grable. In **75** she is the blond at the left of the star line-up, which continues with Johnny Downs, Patsy Kelly, Jack Haley, Tony Martin and Dixie Dunbar; the film, in which Judy Garland made her feature debut, was directed by David Butler. In **76** she is seen with Dan Dailey in *Mother Wore Tights* (directed by Walter Lang).

77 & 78. Vivienne Segal. In **77** she is seen with Walter Pidgeon in *Viennese Nights* (directed by Alan Crosland); the score was by Sigmund Romberg (lyrics by Oscar Hammerstein II); Alexander Gray was the leading man. In **78** she is seen with Walter Woolf in *Golden Dawn* (directed by Ray Enright).

79–81. Ann Sothern. In **79** she is seen with Lanny Ross in *Melody in Spring* (1934; directed by Norman McLeod). In **80** she is seen with Ben Blue, Red Skelton and Rags Ragland in *Panama Hattie* (1942; also directed by McLeod); Ethel Merman did the role on the stage. In **81** she is seen with George Murphy in *Kid Millions* (1934; directed by Roy Del Ruth).

82. Ruth Etting and Gene Austin; the director was Karl Freund.

83. Martha Raye, with Ole Olsen and Chic Johnson (left) in *Hellzapoppin'* (directed by Henry C. Potter).

84. Betty Hutton (as the historical Annie Oakley), seen with Keenan Wynn, Louis Calhern (as the historical "Buffalo Bill," William F. Cody) and Howard Keel in *Annie Get Your Gun* (1950; directed by George Sidney). Ethel Merman had the role on Broadway. The composer was Irving Berlin.

85. Helen Kane and Victor Moore. The 1930 film was directed by Victor Schertzinger, and also starred Buddy (Charles) Rogers. The cartoon character was Betty Boop.

86. Kate Smith, seen with Julia Swayne Gordon, in *Hello, Everybody!* (1933; directed by William Seiter). The leading man was Randolph Scott.

87. Lilian Harvey in *I Am Suzanne* (1934; directed by Rowland V. Lee); Gene Raymond was the leading man.

88. Miliza Korjus, seen with Fernand Gravet (Gravey), Hugh Herbert and Luise Rainer, in *The Great Waltz* (1938; directed by Julien Duvivier).

89. Vivian Blaine, June Haver and Vera-Ellen in *Three Little Girls in Blue* (1946; directed by H. Bruce Humberstone).

90. Judy Canova, seen with John Hubbard, Joe E. Brown (with the "R. V.") and Gus Schilling. The 1943 film was directed by Joseph Santley.

91. Lyda Roberti and Joe Penner in *College Rhythm* (1934; directed by Norman Taurog). The male singing star was Lanny Ross.

92. Wini(fred) Shaw and James Melton. The 1937 film was directed by Louis King.

93. Doris Day, seen with Page Cavanaugh and Lloyd Pratt, in *Romance on the High Seas* (1948; directed by Michael Curtiz). Jack Carson and Janis Paige were starred.

94. Jane Powell, seen with Bonita Granville, in *Song of the Open Road* (directed by S. Sylvan Simon). Edgar Bergen and W. C. Fields were in the cast.

95 & 96. Rudy Vallee. In **95** he is seen with Sally Blane and Charles Sellon in *The Vagabond Lover* (1929; directed by Marshall Neilan). The other performers shown in **96** are Ann Dvorak and Ned Sparks; the 1935 film was directed by Alfred E. Green.

97 & 98. Donald O'Connor. In **97** he is seen with Bing Crosby and Fred MacMurray in *Sing You Sinners* (1938; directed by Wesley Ruggles); Ellen Drew was the female lead. In **98** he is seen with Peggy Ryan; the 1944 film was directed by Charles Lamont.

99 & 100. Cliff Edwards. In **99** he is seen with Charles King (at the left) and Conrad Nagel in *The Hollywood Revue of 1929* (1929; directed by Charles Reisner). In **100** he is seen with Elliott Nugent (in white shirt and bowtie) and Robert Montgomery (sitting on table); Ray Cooke is holding the ace of clubs; Delmer Daves is leaning on the piano; the film is *So This Is College* (1929; directed by Sam Wood); Sally Starr was the female lead.

101 & 102. Danny Kaye. In **101** he is seen with Vera-Ellen in *Wonder Man* (1945; directed by Bruce Humberstone); Virginia Mayo was also in the cast. In **102** he is seen with (Zizi) Jeanmaire in *Hans Christian Andersen* (1952; directed by Charles Vidor); Farley Granger was also in the cast; Frank Loesser wrote words and music.

103 & 104. Eddie Cantor. In **103** he is seen with Spencer Charters in *Whoopee* (1930; directed by Thornton Freeland). In **104** he is seen with Charlotte Greenwood in *Palmy Days* (1931; directed by Edward Sutherland).

105. Nino Martini, seen with Ida Lupino, in *The Gay Desperado* (1936).

106. Russ Columbo, seen with June Knight and Roger Pryor, in *Wake Up and Dream* (1934; directed by Kurt Neumann).

107. Dean Martin, seen with Judy Holliday, in *Bells Are Ringing* (1960; directed by Vincente Minnelli).

108. Mario Lanza, seen with J. Carroll Naish and Kathryn Grayson, in *The Toast of New Orleans* (1950; directed by Norman Taurog).

109. Harry Belafonte, seen with Dorothy Dandridge, in *Carmen Jones* (1954; directed by Otto Preminger).

110. Tony Martin, seen with André Kostelanetz. The 1940 film was directed by Joseph Santley. Rita Hayworth was also starred.

111. Bobby Breen, seen with May Robson, in *Rainbow on the River* (1936; directed by Kurt Neumann).

112. Morton Downey, seen with Beryl Mercer. The 1929 film was directed by Bradley Barker.

113. Elvis Presley. This 1957 film was directed by Hal Kanter. Also featured were Lizabeth Scott and Wendell Corey. Presley's first film was *Love Me Tender*.

114. John Boles. The 1930 film was directed by John Murray Anderson. The other song was "It Happened in Monterey."

115 & 116. Ann Miller. In **115** she is seen with Cyd Charisse and Ricardo Montalban in *The Kissing Bandit* (directed by Laslo Benedek); the big song is "Love Is Where You Find It." In **116** she is seen with Jules Munshin in *On the Town* (1949; directed by Gene Kelly and Stanley Donen); the Broadway show was composed by Leonard Bernstein (lyrics by Betty Comden and Adolph Green); the other sailors were played by Gene Kelly and Frank Sinatra.

117. Jessie Matthews. *Head Over Heels* (1937) was directed by Sonnie Hale. She performed "Dancing on the Ceiling" in *Evergreen*.

118. Bill Robinson, seen with Jennie LeGon. The 1935 film was directed by Walter Lang. Fats Waller was in it. Ann Sothern and Gene Raymond were the stars.

119. Hal LeRoy, seen with Rochelle Hudson. The 1934 film was directed by Murray Roth.

120. Leaping, left to right: Tommy Rall, Matt Mattox and Marc Platt. The film is *Seven Brides for Seven Brothers* (directed by Stanley Donen). The singing stars were Howard Keel and Jane Powell.

121 & 122. *The Goldwyn Follies* (1938; directed by George Marshall). The two greatest songs are "Love Walked In" and "Our Love Is Here to Stay." In the foreground of **121**: Jerome Cowan, Vera Zorina and Phil Baker. In **122**: Kenny Baker and Helen Jepson.

123. Judy Garland and Mickey Rooney in *Girl Crazy* (directed by Norman Taurog).

124. *The Shocking Miss Pilgrim* (1947; directed by George Seaton). In the still: Dick Haymes, Betty Grable and Gene Lockhart. Betty Grable played a typist (or "typewriter").

125. Audrey Hepburn in *Funny Face* (1957; directed by Stanley Donen). Fred Astaire was the male lead.

126. *Rhapsody in Blue* (1945; directed by Irving Rapper). In the still: Al Jolson, Robert Alda, Charles Coburn.

127. Jeanette MacDonald and Ramon Novarro in *The Cat and the Fiddle* (1934; directed by William K. Howard). "I've Told Ev'ry Little Star" is from *Music in the Air*.

128. *Music in the Air* (1934; directed by Joe May). In the still, left to right: Al Shean, June Lang, John Boles, Reginald Owen, Gloria Swanson and Douglass Montgomery.

129. *I Dream Too Much* (1935; directed by John Cromwell). Left to right: Eric Blore, Lily Pons, Henry Fonda.

130. *Sweet Adeline* (1935; directed by Mervyn LeRoy). Helen Morgan starred on Broadway. In the still: Wini(fred) Shaw, Hugh Herbert, Donald Woods, Ned Sparks.

131 & 132. *Show Boat* (directed by James Whale). Shown in **131** are Helen Morgan, Hattie McDaniel and Irene Dunne; in **132**, Paul Robeson (Allan Jones and Irene Dunne are on the posters). Cap'n Andy was played by Charles Winninger.

133. *Can't Help Singing* (directed by Frank Ryan). In the still: Robert Paige, Deanna Durbin and Thomas Gomez. "Spring Will Be . . ." is from *Christmas Holiday*.

134. *Centennial Summer* (1946; directed by Otto Preminger). The adults, left to right: Cornel Wilde, Jeanne Crain, Dorothy Gish, Walter Brennan, Linda Darnell and William Eythe.

135. *Hot Heiress* (directed by Clarence Badger). Left to right: Ben Lyon, Ona Munson, Tom Dugan and Inez Courtney.

136. *The Boys from Syracuse* (1940; directed by Edward Sutherland). Seated: Irene Hervey, Allan Jones and Rosemary Lane. Standing: Martha Raye and Joe Penner.

137. Dana Andrews and Jeanne Crain singing "It's a Grand Night for Singing" in *State Fair* (1945; directed by Walter Lang); Dick Haymes and Vivian Blaine were also in the cast. The winning song was "It Might As Well Be Spring." The 1933 film starred Will Rogers and Janet Gaynor. The 1962 film starred Pat Boone, Bobby Darin, Pamela Tiffin and Ann-Margret.

138. Yul Brynner and Deborah Kerr in *The King and I* (1956; directed by Walter Lang). The locale is Siam. The roles were played by Brynner and Gertrude Lawrence on Broadway.

139. Gordon MacRae and Shirley Jones in *Oklahoma!* (1955; directed by Fred Zinnemann). On the stage the stars were Alfred Drake and Joan Roberts.

140. Daniel L. Haynes in *Hallelujah*. The female lead was Nina Mae McKinney.

141. Irving Berlin singing "Oh, How I Hate to Get Up in the Morning" in *This Is the Army* (1943; directed by Michael Curtiz).

George Murphy and Joan Leslie were also in the cast. The 1918 show was *Yip, Yip, Yaphank*.

142. Harry Richman in *Puttin' On the Ritz* (directed by Edward H. Sloman). Joan Bennett and James Gleason were also in the cast.

143 & 144. *Born to Dance* (1936; directed by Roy Del Ruth). In **143**: Frances Langford and Buddy Ebsen; in **144**, Eleanor Powell. "I've Got You . . ." was sung by Virginia Bruce.

145. Also from *Born to Dance*. Eleanor Powell is the soloist. James Stewart was the leading man.

146 & 147. *Rosalie* (1937; directed by W. S. Van Dyke). The leading man was Nelson Eddy. The two most important songs were "Rosalie" and "In the Still of the Night."

148. *Night and Day* (1946; directed by Michael Curtiz). In the still: Cary Grant, Mary Martin and Jane Wyman. Alexis Smith was the leading lady. The show that made Mary Martin famous was *Leave It to Me*.

149. *Good News* (directed by Nick Grinde and Edgar J. MacGregor). Left to right: Gus Shy, Bessie Love and Delmer Daves. The 1947 remake starred June Allyson and Peter Lawford.

150 & 151. *Just Imagine* (directed by David Butler). Shown in **150** are Marjorie White and Frank Albertson.

152 & 153. *Sunny Side Up* (1929; directed by David Butler). The heroine was Janet Gaynor; the hero, Charles Farrell; they were first teamed in *Seventh Heaven*. The song in **153** is "Turn On the Heat"; the performer is Sharon Lynn.

154 & 155. Jimmy Durante. "Inka Dinka Doo" is from *Joe Palooka*. In **154** Durante is seen with George M. Cohan in *The Phantom President* (1932; directed by Norman Taurog); Claudette Colbert was the leading lady. In **155** he is seen with Rudy Vallee and Cliff Edwards; the film was directed by George White, Thornton Freeland and Harry Lachman; Alice Faye made her debut in it.

156. Jack Oakie in *Hit the Deck* (directed by Luther Reed).

157. Left to right: Louise Fazenda, Frank Fay, Beatrice Lillie and Lloyd Hamilton. The film was directed by John Adolfi.

158. Bert Lahr and Charlotte Greenwood. The film was directed by Charles Reisner.

159. Robert Woolsey (with cigar) and Bert Wheeler in *Cockeyed Cavaliers* (1934; directed by Mark Sandrich). Thelma Todd is holding the fan, Dorothy Lee is pointing.

160. Mitzi Green. (The revue had many directors.)

161–163. The film in **161** is *A Day at the Races* (1937; directed by Sam Wood); Margaret Dumont is being restrained by Sig Rumann; the brothers, left to right, are Harpo, Groucho and Chico. **162** shows Oscar Shaw and Mary Eaton in *The Cocoanuts* (1929; directed by Robert Florey); the song was "When My Dreams Come True." **163**

shows Kitty Carlisle and Allan Jones (with Sig Rumann) in *A Night at the Opera* (1935; directed by Sam Wood).

164. The Nicholas Brothers (Fayard and Harold) in *Sun Valley Serenade* (1941; directed by H. Bruce Humberstone). Glenn Miller's band played, Tex Beneke sang. The stars were Sonja Henie and John Payne.

165. The Boswell Sisters—Martha, Connee (Connie) and Helvetia (Vet)—in *Moulin Rouge* (1934; directed by Sidney Lanfield). The stars were Constance Bennett and Franchot Tone.

166. The Mills Brothers (Herbert, Donald, Harry and John, Jr.) with Jimmy Durante and Lupe Velez. The 1934 film was directed by Elliott Nugent.

167. The Ritz Brothers (Al, Harry and Jimmy) and the Andrews Sisters (Maxene, Patty and LaVerne) in *Argentine Nights* (1940; directed by Albert S. Rogell).

168. June Haver (as Marilyn Miller) and Ray Bolger in *Look for the Silver Lining* (1949; directed by David Butler). The song was by Jerome Kern (lyrics by Bud DeSylva), and was performed by Marilyn Miller in *Sally*. Marilyn Miller appeared in the film versions of *Sally* and *Sunny* and in the movie *Her Majesty, Love*.

169. Ann Sheridan (right) portrayed Nora Bayes, and Dennis Morgan (standing) portrayed Jack Norworth. The 1944 film was directed by David Butler. Also in the still are Marie Wilson and Jack Carson.

170. *Three Little Words* (1950; directed by Richard Thorpe). Left to right: Fred Astaire (as Kalmar), Gloria De Haven, Red Skelton (as Ruby) and Keenan Wynn. "Three Little Words" is from *Check and Double Check*.

171. Larry Parks (standing) as Al Jolson in *The Jolson Story* (1946; directed by Alfred E. Green). Seated: Tamara Shayne, Evelyn Keyes, Ludwig Donath.

172. John McCormack and Maureen O'Sullivan in *Song O' My Heart* (directed by Frank Borzage). Alice Joyce was the female lead.

173. Lauritz Melchior, seen with Andrew Tombes, in *Two Sisters from Boston* (1946; directed by Henry Koster).

174. Grace Moore and Franchot Tone in *The King Steps Out* (1936). The songs were by Fritz Kreisler (lyrics by Dorothy Fields); the revised song was "Stars in My Eyes."

175. Grace Moore and Lawrence Tibbett in *New Moon* (directed by John Conway). The 1940 version starred Jeanette MacDonald and Nelson Eddy. The composer was Sigmund Romberg.

176. Bessie Love, Charles King and Anita Page in *The Broadway Melody* (1929; directed by Harry Beaumont). "Happy Days . . ." is from *Chasing Rainbows*.

177. Marie Dressler in *The Hollywood Revue of 1929* (directed by Charles Reisner).

178 & 179. The cartoon shown in **178** is *Three Little Pigs* (1933); the song is "Who's Afraid of the Big Bad Wolf?" **179** is from *Dumbo*; the mouse's voice was that of Edward Brophy.

180. Reginald Denny, Kay Johnson and Roland Young in *Madam Satan* (1930).

181. *Black Orpheus* (*Orfeu Negro*; 1959; directed by Marcel Camus). Filmed in Rio de Janeiro. The actress in the still is Lea Garcia. The leading roles were played by Marpessa Dawn and Bruno Mello.

182. Myrna Loy. The film was directed by Roy Del Ruth. The leading lady was Carlotta King. "The Red Shadow" was played by John Boles in 1929, Dennis Morgan in 1943 and Gordon MacRae in 1953.

183. Dolores Del Rio in *In Caliente* (1935; directed by Lloyd Bacon). The leading man was Pat O'Brien.

184. *The Great Ziegfeld* (directed by Robert Z. Leonard). The stars were William Powell, Luise Rainer and Myrna Loy.

185 & 186. The dance in **185** is from *Honolulu* (1939; directed by Edward Buzzell); leading man, Robert Young. **186** is from *Broadway Melody of 1938* (1937; directed by Roy Del Ruth); leading man, Robert Taylor; note the neon sign at the right reading "Broadway Melody 1937."

187. Constance Bennett in *Moulin Rouge* (1934; directed by Sidney Lanfield). The male lead was Franchot Tone.

188. *Yankee Doodle Dandy*, a biography of George M. Cohan (1942; directed by Michael Curtiz). Left to right: Jeanne Cagney, James Cagney (as Cohan), Joan Leslie, Walter Huston and Rosemary De Camp. The song is "You're a Grand Old Flag."

189. Hal Skelly in *The Dance of Life* (directed by John Cromwell).

190. Irene Bordoni and Jack Buchanan in *Paris* (directed by Clarence Badger).

191. W. C. Fields and Marilyn Miller in *Her Majesty, Love* (directed by William Dieterle). The male lead was Ben Lyon.

192. Gertrude Lawrence, seen with Charles Ruggles and Arthur Treacher. The 1929 film was directed by Robert Florey.

193. Ethelind Terry, seen with Charles Kaley, in *Lord Byron of Broadway* (1930; directed by William Nigh and Harry Beaumont).

194. Norma Terris and J. Harold Murray. The 1929 film was directed by Marcel Silver.

195. Left to right: Lilyan Tashman, Ann Pennington, Nick Lucas, Winnie Lightner and Nancy Welford in *Gold Diggers of Broadway* (directed by Roy Del Ruth).

196. Mae West in *I'm No Angel* (1933; directed by Wesley Ruggles). The male lead was Cary Grant.

197. Marilyn Monroe and Jane Russell in *Gentlemen Prefer Blondes* (1953; directed by Howard Hawks). Carol Channing was the stage star.

198. Fred MacMurray and June Haver in *Where Do We Go from Here?* (1945; directed by Gregory Ratoff).

199. Esther Williams and Van Johnson in *Easy to Wed* (1946; directed by Edward Buzzell).

200–202. Nancy Carroll. In **200** she is seen with Buddy (Charles) Rogers in *Follow Thru* (1930; directed by Laurence Schwab and Lloyd Corrigan). In **201** she is seen with Hal Skelly in *The Dance of Life* (1929; directed by John Cromwell). In **202** she is seen with Jobyna Howland and Stanley Smith in *Honey* (1930; directed by Wesley Ruggles).

203. Colleen Moore, seen with Fredric March and (at the left) Virginia Lee Corbin. The film was directed by William A. Seiter.

204 & 205. Marion Davies. Lawrence Gray is the leading man seen in both stills. **204** is from *The Florodora Girl* (1930; directed by Harry Beaumont). **205** is from *Marianne* (1929; directed by Robert Z. Leonard).

206. Sue Carol, Sid Silvers and Grant Withers. The 1930 film was directed by Ray Enright.

207. Leopold Stokowski (center), seen with Adolphe Menjou (right). The soprano was Deanna Durbin. This 1937 film was directed by Henry Koster. Stokowski appeared with Mickey Mouse in *Fantasia*.

208. Left to right: Chill Wills, William Gaxton, Lucille Ball and Tommy Dix in *Best Foot Forward* (1943; directed by Edward Buzzell). The school song is "Buckle Down, Winsocki."

209. Hermione Gingold, Louis Jourdan and Leslie Caron in *Gigi* (1958; directed by Vincente Minnelli). Maurice Chevalier appeared in the film. The songs were by Frederick Loewe (lyrics by Alan Jay Lerner). The original short story was by Colette. The song "Gigi" won the Academy Award.

Index of Performers

Only those performers actually shown in the stills are indexed. The numbers are those of the stills
*(stills **A** through **F** appear on the covers).*

Index of Performers

Index of Films

Only the films for which there are stills are indexed. The numbers are those of the stills
(stills **A** through **F** appear on the covers).